STECK-VAUGHN

# Comprehension Skills

# FACTS

## LEVEL
## E

Linda Ward Beech
Tara McCarthy
Donna Townsend

STECK-VAUGHN
COMPANY
A Subsidiary of National Education Corporation

| | |
|---|---|
| *Executive Editor:* | Diane Sharpe |
| *Project Editor:* | Melinda Veatch |
| *Senior Editor:* | Anne Rose Souby |
| *Design Coordinator:* | Sharon Golden |
| *Project Design:* | Howard Adkins Communications |
| *Cover Illustration:* | Rhonda Childress |
| *Photographs:* | ©Bruce Van Patter |

ISBN 0-8114-7849-1

7 8 9 0 VP 02 01 00 99 98

Facts are things like names, dates, and places. In this book you will practice finding facts.

Facts are all around you. Have you noticed flowers? When do they bloom? Have you noticed people's faces? Are they happy or sad? Noticing facts helps you enjoy the world around you. What facts can you see in the picture on this page?

# What Are Facts?

Facts are sometimes called details. They are small pieces of information. Facts can appear in true stories, such as those in the newspaper. Facts can also appear in legends and other stories that people make up.

## How to Read for Facts

You can find facts by asking yourself questions. Ask *who*, and your answer will be a fact about a person. Ask *what*, and your answer will be a fact about a thing. Ask *where*, and your answer will be a fact about a place. Ask *when*, and your answer will be a fact about a time. Ask *how many* or *how much*, and your answer will be a fact about a number or an amount.

## Try It!

Read this story and look for facts as you read. Ask yourself *how many* and *what*.

◆

### Snakes

If you're afraid of snakes, maybe it's because you don't know much about these interesting animals. There are more than 2,700 different kinds of snakes. They live on every continent of the world except Antarctica. They come in all sizes. The largest snake ever measured was a python that was 32 feet long. One of the smallest is the thread snake, which is only about 4 inches long.

Did you find these facts when you read the paragraph? Write the facts on the lines below.

◆ How many different kinds of snakes are there?

   *Fact:* _____

◆ What is one of the smallest snakes?

   *Fact:* _____

**To check your answers, turn to page 62.**

# Practice Finding Facts

Below are some practice questions. The first two are already answered. Answer the third one on your own.

_B_    **1.** The thread snake is

     **A.** 4 feet long        **C.** 32 feet long
     **B.** 4 inches long      **D.** 32 inches long

Look at the question and answers again. The word _long_ is asking for a number. There are many numbers in the paragraph, but you are looking for one that describes the length of the thread snake. Read the paragraph until you find the words _thread snake_. You should find this sentence: "One of the smallest is the thread snake, which is only about 4 inches long." So **B** is the correct answer. Answer **C** is also a fact from the story, but it describes pythons, not thread snakes.

_C_    **2.** The continent that has no snakes is

     **A.** Africa        **C.** Antarctica
     **B.** Australia      **D.** America

Look at the question. It asks for the name of a _continent_ that has no snakes. Search the story about snakes for the name of a continent. You should find this sentence: "They live on every continent of the world except Antarctica." The words are a little different from the words in the story. But "except Antarctica" tells you that Antarctica has no snakes. So the answer is **C**.

Now it's your turn to practice. Answer the next question by writing the letter of the correct answer on the line.

_____ **3.** The largest snake ever measured was

     **A.** a python        **C.** a thread snake
     **B.** a continent snake    **D.** an Antarctic snake

**To check your answer, turn to page 62.**

# *Using What You Know*

Read the following question words and facts that answer the questions. Ask yourself the questions. Then write facts about yourself on the lines.

### *Who?*
Dian Fossey lived with gorillas for 18 years.
Michelangelo was a great Italian artist.

◆ My name is _____ .

### *What?*
Halley's comet is visible every 76 years.
The Indian blanket is a red and yellow flower.

◆ My favorite song is _____ .

### *Where?*
Black holes are dead stars in space.
The first passenger elevator was built in New York City.

◆ I live in the city of _____ .

### *When?*
Football season starts in the fall.
The store opens at 9:00.

◆ I was born on _____ , 19 _____ .

### *How Many?/How Much?*
A brown bear can weigh more than a horse.
Louisville won 20 of its last 22 games.

◆ There are _____ students in my class.

# How to Use This Book

In this book you will read 25 stories. Each story has two parts. Read the first part, then answer five questions about it. Then read the second part and answer the next five questions.

When you finish reading each story and answering the questions about it, check your answers by looking at pages 59 through 61. Write the number of correct answers in the score box at the top of the page. After you finish all the stories, turn to pages 56 through 58. Work through "Think and Apply." The answers to those questions are on page 62.

## Remember

This book asks questions about facts in stories. When you answer the questions, use the facts in the story. You may already know some facts about the subject, but the story will have the answers you need for the questions.

## Hints for Better Reading

◆ Look for facts while you are reading the stories. Notice the names of people, animals, and things. Look for places, dates, and times.

◆ Read each question carefully. Think about the facts you need to answer the question. Try to find a sentence in the story that has some of the same words as the question.

◆ Try to remember the facts you read in the story. If you can't remember, look back at the story.

## Challenge Yourself

Try this special challenge. Read each story. Cover the story with a sheet of paper, and try to remember the facts. Answer the questions without looking back at the story.

## Where There's Smoke, There's a Message

People have always found ways to send messages. In early days people beat sticks against hollow logs. Others in nearby villages heard these sounds. The messages gave warnings and told of important events such as wars, changes in leaders, and festivals and celebrations. Later, people stretched animal skins over gourds to make drums.

Other people used smoke signals and signal fires. Smoke signals were made by releasing puffs of white smoke into the air. But smoke could not be seen at night. So in the dark, people lit signal fires at certain points along a route, perhaps on mountaintops. The fires signaled events such as the birth of a king.

_____ **1.** In early days people beat sticks against
    A. caves      C. the ground
    B. logs      D. bushes

_____ **2.** Later, people stretched animal skins over
    A. holes      C. streams
    B. trees      D. gourds

_____ **3.** Puffs of smoke released into the air were called
    A. smoke signals      C. drum messages
    B. signal fires      D. hollow logs

_____ **4.** Signal fires were sometimes lit
    A. in caves      C. on mountaintops
    B. below rocks      D. in rivers

_____ **5.** Fires lit at certain points along a route told of
    A. travels      C. smoke
    B. events      D. signals

In the 1700s people thought of a new way to send messages. They set up relay stations two or three miles apart. They placed a tall post at each station. The top of each post could be seen at the next stations. By pulling ropes, people moved three hinged arms at the top of the posts. In different positions, the arms signaled different coded letters. The system worked well. In 1806 a message traveled one hundred miles in three minutes.

Even before electricity, people flashed lights to send messages. On sunny days soldiers polished their shields. Then they flashed the rays of the sun off the shields to soldiers on the next hill. In the nineteenth century, mirrors were used to do this job. This was the basis for Morse code, which is still used today.

_____ **6.** In the 1700s people thought of a new way to
   **A.** pull ropes          **C.** polish shields
   **B.** travel swiftly       **D.** share information

_____ **7.** Every two or three miles, people put up a
   **A.** pole          **C.** light
   **B.** code          **D.** hill

_____ **8.** When the ropes were pulled, they
   **A.** flashed a light    **C.** caught the sun's rays
   **B.** made a noise       **D.** moved hinged arms

_____ **9.** To send messages, early soldiers used
   **A.** electricity    **C.** shiny shields
   **B.** Morse code     **D.** flashlights

_____ **10.** Later, people used mirrors
   **A.** to send signals    **C.** as shields
   **B.** to fight wars      **D.** as weapons

Many people think that an octopus makes a curious sight. It has eight arms coming out of a rounded head. Its name, *octopus*, comes from two Greek words that mean "eight feet."

People once thought that the octopus was a "devilfish" or a "monster of the sea." They thought that an octopus had arms long enough to hug a whole ship. But experts today know that this is not true. These odd sea creatures actually prefer to be left alone. And even the largest type of octopus is too small to hug a ship. Their average length is only about ten feet. Most kinds are not any larger than a person's fist. However, an octopus that feels threatened *will* bite, using its sharp, parrot-like beak. Also, every once in a while, an octopus will "hug" a diver.

_____ **1.** An octopus has
- **A.** six arms
- **B.** four arms
- **C.** eight arms
- **D.** two arms

_____ **2.** People once thought that the octopus was a
- **A.** mammal
- **B.** monster
- **C.** whale
- **D.** pet

_____ **3.** The octopus likes to
- **A.** be left alone
- **B.** play with people
- **C.** attack people
- **D.** swim beside boats

_____ **4.** The average length of an octopus is
- **A.** twelve feet
- **B.** thirty feet
- **C.** ten feet
- **D.** fifty feet

_____ **5.** Octopuses have parrot-like
- **A.** wings
- **B.** beaks
- **C.** eyes
- **D.** tails

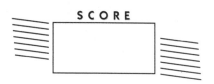
Even though it cannot pull ships under the sea, an octopus can use its arms to move rocks much heavier than itself. Its arms can also handle tiny objects quite well. In one study scientists placed food in screw-top jars for an octopus. The octopus unscrewed the lid and then ate the food from the jar.

An octopus uses its arms mainly to gather food. It eats shellfish, including clams, crabs, and lobsters. It leaves its den at the bottom of the sea at night. When an octopus finds a crab or something else good to eat, it releases poison into the water. This makes the victim easy to catch. For the trip home, the octopus gathers the food into the skin between its arms. This area is called the web. When its web is full, the octopus returns home for a fine meal.

_____ **6.** An octopus will use its arms to
   **A.** pull ships down    **C.** poison a crab
   **B.** attack people    **D.** move large objects

_____ **7.** When given a screw-top jar, an octopus will probably
   **A.** break it    **C.** swallow it
   **B.** open it    **D.** look at it

_____ **8.** An octopus uses its arms mainly to
   **A.** eat    **C.** move rocks
   **B.** fight    **D.** carry young

_____ **9.** The octopus carries its food in
   **A.** its mouth    **C.** a layer of skin
   **B.** its beak    **D.** its arms

_____ **10.** The octopus eats its meals
   **A.** above its den    **C.** away from home
   **B.** in its den    **D.** while swimming

You may not know it, but you have probably seen a horse wearing make-up. Making movies is a tricky business. Cameras make things on the screen look different from the way they look in real life. So people who make movies have to use special make-up to keep the actors from looking odd. This goes for animal actors, too. Before a shoot, make-up experts might powder a horse's nose and put mascara on its lashes. Believe it or not, make-up makes the horse look more natural on screen!

Wearing make-up might be the worst thing that a horse has to do while making a movie. The American Humane Association protects horses used in movies. Members of the group are on movie sets to see that the horses are taken care of properly. They make sure that the animals are not mistreated.

_____ **1.** Movie cameras make things look
- **A.** scary
- **B.** lifelike
- **C.** different
- **D.** the same

_____ **2.** A horse in a movie might wear
- **A.** lipstick
- **B.** powder
- **C.** eye shadow
- **D.** perfume

_____ **3.** The people who put make-up on horses are the
- **A.** producers
- **B.** directors
- **C.** make-up experts
- **D.** sound people

_____ **4.** Make-up helps actors look
- **A.** odd
- **B.** worse
- **C.** mistreated
- **D.** natural

_____ **5.** The American Humane Association
- **A.** sells horses
- **B.** films horses
- **C.** protects horses
- **D.** mistreats horses

Animals on a movie set are protected from being hurt during exciting scenes. Have you ever seen a horse run at a full gallop for miles and miles in a movie? The horse really ran for shorter distances and was filmed each time. When the film is shown, it looks as though the horse ran a long distance. If guns are fired during a scene, the horse may have cotton in its ears for protection.

Horses also do stunts in movies. They must be specially trained. You may have seen horses fall through walls, glass windows, or even barbed-wire fences. There is no need to worry about the horses. Moviemakers use special props for such stunts. The walls are made of soft wood. The wire in the fences is really rubber. And the glass in the windows is made from sugar. This is one reason that making movies is so expensive. Most special props can be used only once. Then new ones must be built.

_____

_____ **6.** Long-distance runs are made by filming
    **A.** old movies     **C.** shorter runs
    **B.** other animals     **D.** other horses

_____ **7.** Cotton in a horse's ears protects it from
    **A.** dust     **C.** water
    **B.** noise     **D.** heat

_____ **8.** Special props are used instead of
    **A.** fences     **C.** horses
    **B.** people     **D.** carriages

_____ **9.** Windows in movies are sometimes made of
    **A.** plastic     **C.** wood
    **B.** sugar     **D.** rubber

_____ **10.** Most special props can be used
    **A.** only once     **C.** over and over
    **B.** often     **D.** every day

Hooves pound the hard ground. Dry dust fills the air. Suddenly a horse and rider appear. They race toward a small station and pull to a stop. The rider jumps from the panting horse. He dunks his head in a barrel of water to get a drink and cool off. Then he grabs a sack from the horse's back. In seconds the sack is on another horse. The rider leaps on, too, and is gone.

This scene took place many times between April of 1860 and October of 1861. The riders worked for the Pony Express. Their job was to carry mail between Missouri and California. In those days the Pony Express was the fastest way to send mail between these places. There were no cars or planes. Railroads had not yet been built that far west. The distance was 1,966 miles. Pony Express riders could cover it in ten days or fewer.

_____ 1. The Pony Express carried
   A. dust              C. stamps
   B. mail              D. boxes

_____ 2. Riders went between California and
   A. October           C. Missouri
   B. Mississippi       D. Maryland

_____ 3. The riders stopped to change horses at a
   A. garage            C. stable
   B. railroad          D. station

_____ 4. The riders drank water from a
   A. barrel            C. sack
   B. bottle            D. cup

_____ 5. In 1860 and 1861 there were no cars or
   A. railroads         C. horses
   B. planes            D. riders

It took skill and daring to be a Pony Express rider. A rider had to go 10 to 15 miles before changing horses. After 75 miles the rider could rest. Most riders rode 250 miles a day. The miles through the desert were hot and dry. In winter, riders had to make their way through storms. They met many dangers on the trail.

Many of the riders were teenage boys. The youngest was 13. A rider named William Cody was 15. Later, Cody became a famous cowboy known as Buffalo Bill.

By late 1861 a telegraph line was completed across the country. People could now send messages quickly and easily. The days of the Pony Express were soon over. But tales of the riders and their exciting trips live on. They are a colorful part of the nation's past.

_____

_____ 6. In one day most riders covered
   A. 250 miles     C. 75 miles
   B. 275 miles     D. 15 miles

_____ 7. Two problems riders faced were storms and
   A. old age     C. desert heat
   B. fast horses     D. moonlit nights

_____ 8. Many riders were in their
   A. thirties     C. twenties
   B. sixties     D. teens

_____ 9. By 1861 people could send messages by
   A. typewriter     C. telegraph
   B. air mail     D. telephone

_____ 10. The Pony Express lasted
   A. 13 years     C. forever
   B. 15 years     D. a short time

# Ed Weston, Walk, Walk, Walk!

Walking has always been enjoyed by many people. It has also served a purpose. Today people walk for fun and for their health. But before the days of cars and trains, people often had to walk just to get where they needed to go. Back then the pace of life was much slower.

In 1861 Edward Payson Weston walked 443 miles from Boston to Washington, D.C. It took him ten days to make the trip. But he did not mind the long walk because he had an important goal. He wanted to see the new president take office. He didn't make it in time to see that event, but he did make it to the celebration dance that evening. Weston had walked a long way. But that night he still had enough energy to dance in the same room with the nation's new leader, Abraham Lincoln.

_____ 1. Today many people walk for fun and for
    **A.** money       **C.** their health
    **B.** fame        **D.** their jobs

_____ 2. In 1861 Weston walked
    **A.** 443 miles    **C.** 4,430 miles
    **B.** 500 miles    **D.** 43 miles

_____ 3. Weston walked from Boston to
    **A.** Atlanta      **C.** Washington, D.C.
    **B.** Dallas       **D.** Chicago

_____ 4. Weston wanted to see
    **A.** the cherry trees    **C.** the capitol
    **B.** the president      **D.** a museum

_____ 5. Weston danced in the same room with
    **A.** Abraham Lincoln  **C.** Benjamin Franklin
    **B.** Henry Ford       **D.** George Washington

In 1867 Mr. Weston had a different goal. He entered a walking contest to earn money. On this walk he went from Portland, Maine, to Chicago, Illinois. He walked 1,326 miles. It took him 26 days to make the trip. Although Weston won the prize money, he was not satisfied. He felt that he could do much better. Forty years later he proved that he could. He took the same walk and cut his time by 29 hours.

When Weston reached the age of seventy, he decided to celebrate by taking a long walk. In 1909 he walked from New York City to San Francisco in just over 104 days. He covered over 3,800 miles. The following year he returned by walking from Los Angeles to New York City. On this walk he set a new record. He made the trip in just under 77 days.

---

_____ **6.** In 1867 Weston entered a contest to win
    **A.** a trip       **C.** shoes
    **B.** cash       **D.** food

_____ **7.** To walk from Portland to Chicago, Weston took
    **A.** a day       **C.** two weeks
    **B.** a year       **D.** almost a month

_____ **8.** Although he won the prize money, Weston was not
    **A.** healthy       **C.** the winner
    **B.** content       **D.** allowed to finish

_____ **9.** Weston walked to San Francisco to celebrate
    **A.** Halloween       **C.** his birthday
    **B.** Thanksgiving       **D.** his wedding day

_____ **10.** When Weston walked back to New York, his time
    **A.** was worse       **C.** was the same
    **B.** improved       **D.** was not important

# The Rosetta Stone

Many ancient people had forms of writing. Later people studied these old written records to learn about lost ways of life. By the late 1700s, they had learned much about early people and events. But early Egyptian history remained locked in mystery. No one could read the early Egyptian form of writing. It was made up of small pictures. This language was a riddle that no one had solved.

In 1799 Napoleon led his French troops near Rosetta, Egypt. There some of his men found a stone half buried in the mud. The stone was made of black rock. Its flat surface was covered with writing. The writing was divided into three sections. Two parts had Greek words. One part had Egyptian pictures. The pictures were from the ancient language. Experts came from far and near to see the Rosetta stone.

_____ 1. Ancient writings told about
    A. riddles      C. Napoleon
    B. early events      D. the Rosetta stone

_____ 2. No one could read the language of ancient
    A. Egypt      C. France
    B. Greece      D. people

_____ 3. The stone was discovered in
    A. 1700      C. 1799
    B. 1897      D. 1778

_____ 4. The writing on the stone was divided into
    A. three sections      C. five sections
    B. two sections      D. four sections

_____ 5. The pictures on the stone were
    A. Greek      C. English
    B. French      D. Egyptian

The experts guessed that each part of the stone said the same thing. They could read the Greek words, but they could not read the Egyptian picture writing. They hoped that the Greek words would give clues about the Egyptian writing. But no one could break the code.

Years passed, and still no one could tell what the pictures meant. Then in 1818 Jean Francois Champollion studied the stone. He looked at proper names in the Greek writing and found the same names in the Egyptian picture writing. He figured out that some pictures in Egyptian writing stood for sounds. He worked for several more years to solve the mystery. When he finished, he could read the Rosetta stone. In 1822 he wrote a small book about the code. Other people studied his book. Then they could read other writings of ancient Egypt.

_____

_____ **6.** Experts guessed that each part of the stone had the same
     **A.** pictures      **C.** sounds
     **B.** message      **D.** code

_____ **7.** They hoped that the Greek writing would be the
     **A.** key      **C.** right section
     **B.** mystery      **D.** pictures

_____ **8.** Some pictures in Egyptian writing stood for
     **A.** words      **C.** sounds
     **B.** symbols      **D.** whole sentences

_____ **9.** In 1822 Jean Francois Champollion
     **A.** studied the stone      **C.** broke the stone
     **B.** went to France      **D.** wrote a book

_____ **10.** After people studied the book, they were able to read
     **A.** French papers      **C.** Napoleon's letters
     **B.** ancient Egyptian      **D.** Champollion's works

# The Children's Crusade

People have fought over land in the Middle East for centuries. This land is known as the Holy Land. Between 1096 and 1270, many people from Europe went to the Holy Land. They tried to gain control of the area. Even young children had strong feelings about the Holy Land. In 1212 thirty thousand French children decided to take the Holy Land from the people who controlled it. But first they had to get there. Their leader was a shepherd named Stephen. He was only 12 years old. He led them to a town on the coast of France.

They met two sailors, William the Pig and Hugh the Iron. The sailors offered to take them by ship to the Middle East. The sailors did not make them pay money for their voyage. But the children paid in another way.

_____ **1.** The Children's Crusade took place in
    **A.** 1096       **C.** 1270
    **B.** 1212       **D.** 1996

_____ **2.** The children were from
    **A.** France       **C.** Egypt
    **B.** Spain       **D.** the Middle East

_____ **3.** The children wanted to go to
    **A.** England       **C.** Europe
    **B.** France       **D.** the Holy Land

_____ **4.** William the Pig and Hugh the Iron were
    **A.** actors       **C.** sailors
    **B.** teachers       **D.** doctors

_____ **5.** The children did not have to pay money for their
    **A.** food       **C.** clothes
    **B.** voyage       **D.** shoes

William the Pig and Hugh the Iron did not take the children to the Middle East at all. Instead they sailed to the northern coast of Africa. There they sold the children as slaves. The two men made a lot of money for their unusual cargo. But the children were left far from home and far from their goal. They had become the property of strangers.

Some children were taken to Egypt. There some worked for the country's leaders as clerks or errand runners. Others helped the Egyptians speak to the French people who came to trade in Egypt. Only one person, a young priest, was able to get back to France. He told the children's parents and friends what had happened to them. The Children's Crusade was a terrible failure.

_____  **6.** William the Pig and Hugh the Iron did not
  **A.** make money  **C.** keep their word
  **B.** want to leave  **D.** know how to sail

_____  **7.** The sailors went to
  **A.** Africa  **C.** the Middle East
  **B.** France  **D.** the Holy Land

_____  **8.** The children were sold as
  **A.** sailors  **C.** soldiers
  **B.** slaves  **D.** leaders

_____  **9.** Some of the children helped the Egyptians by
  **A.** packing boxes  **C.** sweeping floors
  **B.** writing stories  **D.** speaking French

_____  **10.** The people in France were told about the journey by
  **A.** two children  **C.** only one man
  **B.** a small group  **D.** a woman

Cats first became pets long, long ago. This may have happened as early as 3500 B.C. People in early Egypt loved cats. The cats kept homes free of rats, mice, and snakes. Cats also kept pests away from farms and places where grain was stored.

A thousand years later, cats in Egypt had become more important than ever. They were protected by law. Under the law, people who harmed cats could be put to death. Also during this time, cat owners had a special way to express their sadness when a pet cat died. The owners shaved their eyebrows to show how much they had loved their special pet. Cats even became part of the religion in certain areas of Egypt. In those places people prayed to a goddess of love named Bast. Statues of Bast had a cat's head and a woman's body.

_____ 1. Cats became pets as early as
    **A.** 1000 B.C.    **C.** 3500 B.C.
    **B.** 2000 B.C.    **D.** 5000 B.C.

_____ 2. Cats in early Egypt kept pests away from
    **A.** farms    **C.** streets
    **B.** rats    **D.** trees

_____ 3. People who harmed cats were sometimes
    **A.** put in jail    **C.** given honors
    **B.** cheered    **D.** put to death

_____ 4. When people's cats died, they shaved their
    **A.** heads    **C.** arms
    **B.** eyebrows    **D.** beards

_____ 5. Bast had a cat's
    **A.** legs    **C.** body
    **B.** fur    **D.** head

People in the Far East also loved cats. They used cats to keep mice from nibbling holy books in temples. Cats also kept mice from eating silkworm cocoons. Silk makers traded silk cloth for other fine goods, so they depended on their cats.

Cats in Europe in the 1300s were not treated as well. People killed them by the thousands because they were a symbol of bad luck. This caused the number of rats to grow. Rats carried diseases. A deadly disease called black death spread, killing one fourth of all people in Europe.

Over time people once again learned that cats keep many pests away. By the 1600s cats had again become popular. Settlers arriving in the New World brought cats with them. Some of the cats you know today came from those early cats.

_____ **6.** Cats in the Far East kept mice away from
  **A.** water  **C.** cocoons
  **B.** people  **D.** Europe

_____ **7.** People in Europe in the 1300s thought cats were
  **A.** cute  **C.** good
  **B.** fun  **D.** bad

_____ **8.** With fewer cats the number of rats
  **A.** was larger  **C.** stayed the same
  **B.** was smaller  **D.** was unimportant

_____ **9.** Over one fourth of the people in Europe
  **A.** moved  **C.** owned cats
  **B.** died  **D.** loved cats

_____ **10.** By the 1600s people once again
  **A.** liked cats  **C.** killed cats
  **B.** saved rats  **D.** hated cats

# Steeplejacks

Do you know what a steeplejack is? First you have to know what a steeple is. A steeple is a tower on a church. A steeplejack is someone who repairs steeples. Steeplejacks may also do painting or cleaning.

There is a family of steeplejacks. They travel around the country, finding work as they go. They carry a scrapbook showing the steeples they have repaired. In addition to churches, they work on courthouses and other buildings with towers.

Many of these buildings are old and in need of careful repair. The steeplejacks climb up to look. Often they work with engineers and other experts to decide what to do. Then the family goes to work. Some jobs take a few weeks. Other jobs take months.

_____ 1. A steeple is a church
  A. door        C. tower
  B. bell        D. window

_____ 2. Steeplejacks do painting and
  A. watering    C. preaching
  B. waxing      D. cleaning

_____ 3. Besides fixing churches, steeplejacks sometimes work on
  A. courthouses  C. courtyards
  B. churchyards  D. courtrooms

_____ 4. The first step of a steeplejack's job is to
  A. work for weeks   C. paint the steeple
  B. look at problems  D. clean the steeple

_____ 5. Steeplejacks often work with
  A. engines     C. trains
  B. reporters   D. engineers

Many steeples have lovely clocks on them. Sometimes the golden numbers on the clocks have worn out. The steeplejacks replace the numbers and cover them with thin pieces of gold. Then the clock numbers shine just as they did in the past.

Some steeples have weather vanes on top that need repair. Sometimes the roof of a steeple is worn out. The steeplejacks repair the roofs, too. If a steeple is made of metal, then parts of it may have rusted. The steeplejacks replace these parts. If a steeple is made of wood, then it may need to be painted. Sometimes steeplejacks paint the inside of a steeple, too.

Steeplejacks work in high places and do a lot of climbing. They have to be careful. They don't work in the rain, and they stay home on windy days.

---

_____ **6.** Sometimes steeplejacks have to replace clock
    **A.** hands        **C.** alarms
    **B.** times        **D.** numbers

_____ **7.** Weather vanes on steeples sometimes have to be
    **A.** turned       **C.** repaired
    **B.** blown        **D.** finished

_____ **8.** Sometimes steeplejacks repair
    **A.** roofs        **C.** watches
    **B.** ladders      **D.** bricks

_____ **9.** Steeplejacks do not work in the
    **A.** winter       **C.** steeples
    **B.** clocks       **D.** wind

_____ **10.** In their work steeplejacks need to be very
    **A.** careful      **C.** careless
    **B.** stormy      **D.** windy

Chimpanzees do not have speech organs that allow them to speak. They can make noises, but they cannot say words. They do have hands with four fingers and a thumb, so some chimps have been able to learn Ameslan, American Sign Language. This is the sign language used by some deaf people.

One of the first chimps to learn Ameslan was Washoe. Born in 1965, Washoe began learning to sign words when she was one year old. Like many toddlers, the first "word" she learned was *more*. When she was six, she could use more than 200 signs. Washoe's teachers, Allen and Beatrice Gardner, treated Washoe as their own child. She lived with them in their home, and she did not see other chimpanzees. When she did meet another chimp, she must have thought that it was a strange creature. Her sign for chimp was *bug*.

_____

_____ 1. Chimpanzees do not have
  A. a tongue          C. speech organs
  B. a throat          D. teeth

_____ 2. A sign language used by some deaf people is called
  A. English           C. Washoe
  B. Ameslan           D. Gardner

_____ 3. Washoe's first "word" was
  A. go                C. drink
  B. bug               D. more

_____ 4. When she was six, Washoe could use more than
  A. 200 signs         C. 300 signs
  B. 250 signs         D. 1,000 signs

_____ 5. Washoe probably thought that other chimps were
  A. her teachers      C. strange creatures
  B. her friends       D. deaf people

Lucy is another chimpanzee that learned sign language. She was born a year after Washoe and lived with another family, the Temerlins. The Temerlins taught her to sign, and she learned quickly. She learned to ask for one of her favorite foods by signing the words for *candy drink fruit*. When Lucy did this, the Temerlins knew that she wanted watermelon. Washoe also made up a word for watermelon. She called it *drink fruit*.

The Temerlins and the Gardners have found that chimps are like humans in many ways. Sometimes chimps behave as if they were human. When chimps are joyful, they clap their hands. And when they are angry, they sometimes call their enemies names. They use names they have learned in sign language.

_____ **6.** Lucy was a good
- **A.** student
- **B.** athlete
- **C.** musician
- **D.** teacher

_____ **7.** Both Lucy and Washoe made up a word for
- **A.** drink
- **B.** fruit
- **C.** watermelon
- **D.** candy

_____ **8.** In many ways chimps are like
- **A.** bugs
- **B.** people
- **C.** names
- **D.** their enemies

_____ **9.** When a chimp claps its hands, it is probably
- **A.** angry
- **B.** sad
- **C.** happy
- **D.** thinking

_____ **10.** When a chimp is angry, it might
- **A.** bite
- **B.** swing its arms
- **C.** call others names
- **D.** jump up and down

In pioneer days the coming of a showboat was a big event. It was the only fun for many settlers along the Mississippi and Ohio rivers. There were no movies. A boat bringing singers, dancers, and actors was a big treat.

One of the first groups to perform from a boat was the Chapman family. They floated from town to town on a large, flat boat. The boat was one hundred feet long. After they landed, the Chapmans paraded through the town. They played trumpets and hung posters to announce their show. That night almost everyone in town came to see them.

Tickets cost fifty cents. But instead of paying money, some people traded things they had grown or made. The Chapmans often got fresh berries or homemade bread!

_____ **1.** For many settlers the showboat was their only
    **A.** radio      **C.** appearance
    **B.** parade      **D.** entertainment

_____ **2.** In pioneer days there were no
    **A.** boats      **C.** trumpets
    **B.** movies      **D.** plays

_____ **3.** The Chapman family floated from
    **A.** town to town      **C.** stage to stage
    **B.** boat to boat      **D.** across the ocean

_____ **4.** Tickets cost
    **A.** five cents      **C.** one hundred boats
    **B.** fifty cents      **D.** fifty berries

_____ **5.** Instead of paying money for tickets, some people
    **A.** traded things      **C.** trained actors
    **B.** performed acts      **D.** tricked others

In 1836 the Chapmans bought a steamboat. The steamboat had its own power, so it could go against the flow of the rivers. The Chapmans could visit many more towns.

Soon other showboats were on the rivers, too. Some of the most popular boats had circuses on them. One huge boat was called the *Floating Circus Palace*. It was built in 1851. The *Palace* was big enough to carry forty horses. More than three thousand people at a time could watch a show on the *Palace*.

Gradually people began to move west. The little towns along the rivers grew to be big cities. The people built their own theaters and circuses. Movies were invented. When a showboat arrived, only a few people came to greet it. The last great showboat to float on the rivers was the *Golden Rod*. It stopped giving shows in 1943.

_____

_____ **6.** The Chapmans bought a steamboat in
    **A.** 1863     **C.** 1851
    **B.** 1836     **D.** 1943

_____ **7.** The steamboat made it easier to visit more
    **A.** communities     **C.** acrobats
    **B.** fairs     **D.** currents

_____ **8.** Some of the most popular boats carried
    **A.** famous people     **C.** circus performers
    **B.** floating zoos     **D.** television crews

_____ **9.** The *Floating Circus Palace* was
    **A.** small     **C.** light
    **B.** last     **D.** large

_____ **10.** The *Palace* could hold more than three thousand
    **A.** theaters     **C.** customers
    **B.** horses     **D.** countries

# The Greatest

At age 18 Mildred Ella Didrikson was already on her way to becoming the greatest woman athlete in history. She loved to play baseball. She was nicknamed "Babe" after Babe Ruth, the famous baseball player. She grew up in Beaumont, Texas. In high school Babe was the star of the basketball team. She was also the All-City Champion high diver. She played baseball, football, pool, and tennis. She boxed and swam. In track and field, she won contest after contest. Then she moved to Dallas. There she became the All-American Girls Basketball Champion.

There was only one place left for her to test her skills. At the 1932 Olympic games, the crowd watched in excitement as Babe set new world records. She threw the javelin more than 143 feet. She ran the women's 80-meter hurdles in under 12 seconds. Babe proudly accepted two gold medals.

_____ 1. Mildred Ella Didrikson was
    A. from Canada      C. a great athlete
    B. a movie star      D. a famous writer

_____ 2. Mildred Ella's nickname, "Babe," comes from
    A. a baseball star      C. her friend Sue Ellen
    B. a book she read      D. a basketball champion

_____ 3. Babe was the best high diver in
    A. track      C. the Olympics
    B. Beaumont      D. Dallas

_____ 4. Babe threw the javelin more than
    A. 12 seconds      C. 180 feet
    B. 80 meters      D. 143 feet

_____ 5. At the 1932 Olympics, Babe
    A. hurt her arm      C. won two gold medals
    B. played baseball      D. worked in the field

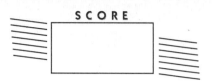
When the Olympics were over, a man named Grantland Rice talked to Babe. Rice was a famous sportswriter. He suggested to Babe that she try a sport that was new to her. He wanted her to play golf! "Well, I'll try it," said Babe, "just for the fun of it." As it turned out, Babe spent most of the rest of her life playing golf. By the time she was 24, she was already a champion player. During one golf tournament, Babe met George Zaharias. They liked one another right away and soon got married. George began managing Babe's career.

Babe became seriously ill with cancer. But the cancer operation didn't stop her from playing golf. She kept winning, and she donated most of her prize money to the American Cancer Society. The disease spread, however. Babe died in Galveston, Texas, in 1956.

---

**6.** Babe tried a new sport after she talked to a
    **A.** writer        **C.** golfer
    **B.** winner      **D.** runner

**7.** Babe met George Zaharias
    **A.** at the Olympics    **C.** at a golf contest
    **B.** in a hospital      **D.** at a business meeting

**8.** George was Babe's
    **A.** writer       **C.** trainer
    **B.** manager     **D.** athlete

**9.** After her operation, Babe
    **A.** started writing    **C.** gave up sports
    **B.** went home       **D.** kept playing golf

**10.** Babe gave the American Cancer Society
    **A.** golf         **C.** trouble
    **B.** sports      **D.** money

# The Myth of Arachne

Athena was the Greek goddess of wisdom. She also taught useful arts to the people of Greece. One of Athena's favorite pupils was a girl named Arachne. Athena taught Arachne how to weave. Arachne was a good pupil and a wonderful weaver. People came from far and wide to see her work.

One day Arachne began to brag about her weaving. She said that she was a better weaver than Athena was. When Athena heard about this, she was not happy. She dressed herself as an old woman and went to see Arachne.

"You are a fine weaver," Athena told Arachne. "But why do you compare yourself to the gods? You should be content to be the best among the humans." Arachne laughed. "Let Athena come here and see who is best," she said.

_____ **1.** Athena was a
    **A.** goddess      **C.** gardener
    **B.** human      **D.** pupil

_____ **2.** Athena taught Arachne how to
    **A.** write      **C.** paint
    **B.** boast      **D.** weave

_____ **3.** One day Arachne began to
    **A.** sing      **C.** brag
    **B.** sew      **D.** cry

_____ **4.** Athena dressed as
    **A.** an old woman      **C.** an old weaver
    **B.** an old artist      **D.** a wise goddess

_____ **5.** Athena asked Arachne why she compared herself to
    **A.** rugs      **C.** girls
    **B.** humans      **D.** gods

Arachne's words made Athena angry. The goddess threw off her costume. "You will have your wish," she told the girl. "Let us begin now."

The two worked away at their looms. Athena wove the most beautiful picture ever seen. It showed the gods in all their glory. The colors and threads in her work were perfect. Arachne also wove perfectly. But Athena was surprised at Arachne's picture. It made fun of the gods.

The goddess grabbed Arachne's weaving and tore it to pieces. Then she hit Arachne with part of the loom. Now it was Arachne's turn to be surprised. Her head became smaller and smaller, and her fingers grew into long, thin legs. The proud Arachne became a spider. "Now you can weave forever," said Athena to the spider.

_____ **6.** Arachne's words made Athena
    **A.** happy        **C.** laugh
    **B.** angry       **D.** sad

_____ **7.** The colors and threads in Athena's picture were
    **A.** not right    **C.** all wrong
    **B.** just right    **D.** almost right

_____ **8.** Arachne's picture did not show
    **A.** gods        **C.** colors
    **B.** skill        **D.** respect

_____ **9.** The goddess was so angry that she
    **A.** shook Arachne    **C.** changed Arachne
    **B.** begged Arachne   **D.** started crying

_____ **10.** Arachne was no longer a
    **A.** weaver      **C.** girl
    **B.** spider      **D.** goddess

Ocean waves pound against the shore. Each wave leaves behind thousands of grains of sand. This sand becomes part of the shore itself. The grains of sand were once part of solid rocks. The rocks were worn down by water and weather into small grains. The wind blows the dry grains of sand into each other and into other objects. Over time the grains are molded into tiny balls. They keep this round shape for millions of years.

In some places strong winds blow the sand into giant hills called sand dunes. If the wind blows from only one direction, sand dunes will slope gently on one side and fall steeply on the other. If the wind changes direction often, dunes might be shaped like giant swirling stars. In a steady wind, sand dunes move and change shape. These moving dunes can completely cover roads and fences.

_____ **1.** An ocean wave leaves behind
  **A.** rocks       **C.** a steady wind
  **B.** stars       **D.** grains of sand

_____ **2.** Over time grains of sand are shaped into
  **A.** tiny balls       **C.** stars
  **B.** tiny cones       **D.** squares

_____ **3.** Sand dunes are formed by
  **A.** stars       **C.** water
  **B.** tides       **D.** winds

_____ **4.** When wind changes direction often, dunes are shaped like
  **A.** rocks       **C.** logs
  **B.** stars       **D.** trees

_____ **5.** Sand dunes move and change shape
  **A.** gently       **C.** in a steady wind
  **B.** steeply       **D.** by solid rocks

The smooth surfaces of sand dunes also change all the time. Birds leave footprints across the sand. Tiny sand crabs leave tracks that barely skim the surface and then vanish into small, deep holes. Winds lift and drop sand into patterns of ripples, and hard rains leave a scattering of tiny craters. If lightning hits sand, it turns it into a solid mass. Plants that can grow on sand dunes hold the sand together when the wind blows.

In some places sand dunes make noises. In Hawaii certain sand dunes make a barking sound. Elsewhere dunes squeak, roar, sing, or boom. The noisy sand dunes have one thing in common. They are made up of grains of sand that are perfectly round, highly polished, and dry. When the sand is moved, the grains rub against each other. This makes the noises.

_____

_____ **6.** Before disappearing into holes, sand crabs
   **A.** jump       **C.** leave a trail
   **B.** sleep      **D.** shed their shell

_____ **7.** When it rains on sand, each drop leaves a
   **A.** noise      **C.** puddle
   **B.** mark      **D.** bird track

_____ **8.** In Hawaii certain sand dunes
   **A.** bark      **C.** squeak
   **B.** roar      **D.** sing

_____ **9.** Sand dunes that make noise have sand that is
   **A.** square      **C.** not wet
   **B.** white      **D.** short

_____ **10.** The noise of a sand dune is caused when the sand
   **A.** gets cold      **C.** turns solid
   **B.** gets wet      **D.** shifts

The wood for baseball bats comes from the ash tree forests of Pennsylvania. Ash wood is especially strong, so it makes good baseball bats. Ash trees are thin compared to other trees. In a high wind, an ash tree can break and fall. However, in the Pennsylvania forests, thicker kinds of trees grow all around the ash trees. These thick trees keep the ash trees from bending too far in a wind storm.

At Slugger Park workers make baseball bats out of ash trees. Workers and their machines can make an ordinary bat in about eight seconds. It takes longer to make a bat for a major-league player. Many of these players want bats that meet their special needs. Once Ted Williams, a famous baseball player, returned some bats to Slugger Park. "The grips just don't feel right to me," he said. The workers measured the grips. Sure enough, Williams was right! The grips were wrong by just a small fraction of an inch.

_____

_____ 1. Baseball bats are made
   A. in wind storms     C. from ash trees
   B. in forests     D. from thick trees

_____ 2. Thick trees protect ash trees from
   A. breaking     C. playing
   B. growing     D. cutting

_____ 3. Workers can make an ordinary bat in about
   A. ten seconds     C. twelve seconds
   B. thirty seconds     D. eight seconds

_____ 4. Many major-league players want bats that are
   A. special     C. stronger
   B. returned     D. longer

_____ 5. When Ted Williams didn't like the grips, he
   A. gave the bats away     C. measured the grips
   B. sent the bats back     D. used the bats anyway

Some players use many bats in a single game. Orlando Cepeda used to throw away a bat after he made a hit with it. He thought that each bat had only a certain number of hits in it. No one could tell how many hits were in a bat. Maybe there was only one. "So why take a chance?" asked Cepeda. When it was his turn to face the pitcher again, he grabbed a brand new Slugger Park bat.

The Slugger Park factory also makes aluminum bats. So far, these are used mostly by college teams and minor-league players. Aluminum bats last longer than wooden ones do. Many baseball fans hope that major-league players will never use these new bats, however. When you hit a ball with one, the sound you hear is a soft *ping*. Fans like their ball games to open with the solid *crack* made by a strong wooden bat. Baseball fans don't like the game to change.

_____

_____ 6. Some players use many bats
- A. over and over
- C. in a single game
- B. for their fans
- D. at the same time

_____ 7. Orlando Cepeda threw away a bat after he
- A. made a hit
- C. faced the pitcher
- B. took a chance
- D. had an idea

_____ 8. Some college teams use
- A. oak bats
- C. fifteen bats
- B. aluminum bats
- D. fans

_____ 9. Many baseball fans don't like
- A. college teams
- C. aluminum bats
- B. pitchers
- D. major-league players

_____ 10. Compared to wooden bats, aluminum bats
- A. feel better
- C. miss balls
- B. break often
- D. last longer

Music recordings are very expensive these days. But there are many ways to save. One way you can get music for less is to borrow records and tapes from a library. But remember to return the library tapes and records when they are due. If you don't, you'll have to pay a fine. Then the music won't be free.

You can also get free music by using swaps or exchanges. Many music stores have a wall chart with information about trading recordings. People list the records and tapes they want to trade. After the title they write *good*, *fair*, or *poor* to let you know the condition of the recording. People have to be honest for this to work.

If you have a blank tape, you can make a copy of a friend's record. Record companies don't like for people to do this. They don't make as much money. But it's not against the law, as long as you do not sell your copy.

_____ **1.** You can borrow records and tapes from
  A. a library        C. the record exchange
  B. a record store   D. a record company

_____ **2.** Record and tape exchange information is for people who
  A. spend money      C. trade music
  B. go to libraries  D. have blank tapes

_____ **3.** The words *good* or *poor* let you know a record's
  A. popularity       C. owner
  B. condition        D. title

_____ **4.** Record companies don't like for people to
  A. pay fines        C. buy tapes
  B. own records      D. copy records

_____ **5.** You are not allowed to record music on tape and
  A. use it           C. sell it
  B. swap it          D. share it

If you have some money to spend on music, you don't have to pay the list price. *List price* is the price that the record company suggests to the music store. Wait for a sale. Sale prices are below list price.

Many music lovers go to yard sales, garage sales, and stores that sell used records. In these places you have to look through stacks and stacks of old records. Usually they aren't sorted. You have to take your time. You might not find anything that interests you at all. But sometimes you'll find a real treasure! You could find a rare record made long ago. You might discover something by a group that is no longer together.

A patient person can build a fine music collection. It doesn't have to take a lot of money. But it does take a lot of time.

---

_____ **6.** The list price is set by the record
  **A.** store          **C.** sale
  **B.** company     **D.** money

_____ **7.** In a sale, records are
  **A.** better         **C.** higher
  **B.** cheaper      **D.** older

_____ **8.** Records at a garage sale are usually
  **A.** new            **C.** in order
  **B.** expensive   **D.** in stacks

_____ **9.** If you're lucky, you may find a used record that is
  **A.** broken        **C.** expensive
  **B.** overdue      **D.** rare

_____ **10.** Building a collection takes a lot of
  **A.** time            **C.** good shape
  **B.** new hits      **D.** money

Today people wear gloves mainly to keep their hands warm. But gloves have had many other uses in the past. Long ago, gloves were a sign of royalty. Kings wore expensive gloves covered with jewels. In Germany a king's glove was hung on a post on market days. The glove stood for the protection of the king. It warned robbers that they would be punished by the king.

Ladies gave one of their gloves to their favorite knight. The knight carried the glove into battle. One story tells of a lady who dropped her glove into a pit of lions. Her brave knight jumped in to get it. Then he threw the glove in the lady's face!

In the 1500s terrible diseases caused many deaths. People wore perfume on their gloves. They hoped that the perfume would keep them from getting these diseases. The perfume also covered up the fact that people did not take baths in those days.

---

_____ **1.** In Germany a king's glove on market day stood for
- **A.** robbers
- **B.** warmth
- **C.** produce
- **D.** protection

_____ **2.** Long ago, ladies gave their gloves to
- **A.** knives
- **B.** lions
- **C.** knights
- **D.** battles

_____ **3.** In the 1500s people wore gloves with
- **A.** perfume
- **B.** dresses
- **C.** leather
- **D.** handkerchiefs

_____ **4.** People thought perfume would protect them from
- **A.** robbers
- **B.** diseases
- **C.** lions
- **D.** knights

_____ **5.** Perfume covered up the fact that people did not
- **A.** take naps
- **B.** take baths
- **C.** take walks
- **D.** use gloves

Many pictures painted long ago show people holding their gloves. Some people believe that this was because gloves didn't fit very well. Gloves made for Queen Elizabeth I are an example. The thumbs on these gloves are five inches long.

Gloves were improved in the 1800s. A Frenchman studied people's hands carefully. Then he made machines that could cut out glove patterns. The Frenchman's gloves fit well. He could also make several pairs at a time. Soon everybody was wearing gloves.

Today there are many kinds of gloves. People wear special gloves for gardening, cooking, driving, and riding bikes. Doctors wear rubber gloves. Some workers wear heavy gloves for protection. Baseball players wear thick leather gloves when they catch the ball. And just about everybody has some warm, woolen gloves for cold days.

_____ **6.** Some people think that early gloves were a poor
     **A.** color       **C.** fit
     **B.** cloth       **D.** buy

_____ **7.** The Frenchman's machines could cut out glove
     **A.** shapes       **C.** shades
     **B.** prices       **D.** circles

_____ **8.** Gloves became available to
     **A.** kings       **C.** Queen Elizabeth
     **B.** everybody       **D.** a Frenchman

_____ **9.** Today doctors wear gloves made of
     **A.** cloth       **C.** leather
     **B.** silk       **D.** rubber

_____ **10.** Factory workers wear heavy gloves for
     **A.** warmth       **C.** safety
     **B.** cooking       **D.** sailing

It was after midnight. A Dutch farmer made one last trip through his greenhouse before going to bed. He walked past rows and rows of tulips. Suddenly he stopped. There, blooming in the early morning hours, was a rare flower. It was a black tulip. In the morning the excited farmer took the tulip to a flower show. By evening the farmer and his prize plant were on television. He was a hero.

Most tulips are red, yellow, white, or pink. A black tulip takes years to develop. The farmer worked on his midnight tulip for seven years. He crossed two dark-purple tulips. They made a seed. The seed took years to grow into a round bulb. Finally a black flower grew from the bulb.

Tulips are a major industry for the Dutch people. Tulip sales bring in millions of dollars. The farmer who grew the midnight tulip could be famous all around the world.

_____

_____ **1.** The farmer made one last trip through his
   **A.** grayhouse          **C.** bath house
   **B.** greenhouse          **D.** pumphouse

_____ **2.** The midnight tulip was
   **A.** dry          **C.** rare
   **B.** red          **D.** late

_____ **3.** The farmer crossed tulips that were
   **A.** pink          **C.** white
   **B.** black          **D.** purple

_____ **4.** Tulip flowers grow from
   **A.** leaves          **C.** roots
   **B.** bulbs          **D.** greenhouses

_____ **5.** For the Dutch people, tulips are a major
   **A.** import          **C.** industry
   **B.** million          **D.** problem

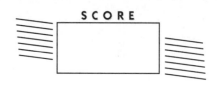
The Dutch people first received tulips in the early 1600s. The tulips came from the Far East. The Dutch loved the beautiful flowers. They were soon growing their own.

People began trying to produce new kinds of tulips. The results were striped tulips, double tulips, and lily tulips. People grew tulips of many new colors. But black tulips were very rare. Someone grew a black tulip in 1891. Another black tulip bloomed in 1955. It was called Queen of the Night.

It may be twenty years before black tulips will grow in ordinary gardens. That's how long it takes to develop bulbs that can be sold. Now the farmer is working on two other unusual tulips. He hopes to grow a tulip that is dark blue. He wants to grow bright green tulips, too.

_____ **6.** Tulips were brought to the Dutch people in
     **A.** 1891      **C.** the 1500s
     **B.** 1955      **D.** the 1600s

_____ **7.** Tulips first came from
     **A.** the Far East      **C.** farmers
     **B.** the Dutch      **D.** queens

_____ **8.** Black tulips bloomed in 1891 and in
     **A.** 1981      **C.** 1595
     **B.** 1955      **D.** 1819

_____ **9.** Developing bulbs to sell takes
     **A.** sixteen years      **C.** ordinary gardens
     **B.** twenty years      **D.** double blooms

_____ **10.** The farmer is working on two other tulips that will be
     **A.** double      **C.** ordinary
     **B.** different      **D.** striped

Two rabbits named Bouqui and Lapin decided to buy a farm together. Lapin, who was always hungry, thought this was a great idea.

"We will divide everything in the garden," said Bouqui. "I will take all the things that grow above the ground, and you can take all the things that grow under the ground. That will be very fair." Lapin thought so, too. The rabbits also agreed how they would divide the work. Bouqui would supply all the seeds for the garden, and Lapin would do the plowing and planting.

The rabbits went to look at the garden every day. At last the crops were ready, and the rabbits could begin to pick them. Bouqui had corn, beans, cabbage, and fine melons. Those were the things above the ground. But Lapin had only roots. Those were the things below the ground. "Don't worry," said Bouqui. "You can feed the roots to our cow."

_____ 1. Bouqui and Lapin decided to buy a
    A. hotel      C. firm
    B. race      D. farm

_____ 2. Bouqui would take all the things
    A. in the garden      C. above the ground
    B. from the house      D. under the ground

_____ 3. Lapin agreed to do the plowing and
    A. watering      C. buying
    B. planting      D. weeding

_____ 4. When the crops were ready, Lapin had only
    A. seeds      C. stems
    B. corn      D. roots

_____ 5. Bouqui told Lapin not to
    A. eat      C. worry
    B. pick      D. sleep

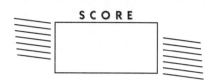
The next spring Lapin said to Bouqui, "I will have all the plants that grow above the ground. It is your turn to have the plants under the ground." Bouqui agreed to Lapin's idea. The rabbits also decided how to share the work again. They would do just what they had done before. Bouqui would supply all the seeds, and Lapin would again do the plowing and planting.

How excited Lapin was when it was time to harvest the garden. But what happened? This year all the good things to eat were below the ground. Bouqui got carrots, turnips, peanuts, and big potatoes. The only things above ground were some gourds. These were for Lapin.

"But these aren't for eating!" cried Lapin. Again Bouqui had to cheer up Lapin. "You can cut out the insides and make fine dippers," Bouqui said.

_____

_____ **6.** The next spring Lapin had a new
    **A.** plan         **C.** rake
    **B.** hose        **D.** plow

_____ **7.** The rabbits agreed that Bouqui would supply the
    **A.** bulbs      **C.** water
    **B.** seeds      **D.** tools

_____ **8.** Lapin was excited when it was time to
    **A.** plow the field    **C.** pick the crops
    **B.** pull the weeds   **D.** plant the seeds

_____ **9.** Lapin's gourds were not
    **A.** good to cut    **C.** above ground
    **B.** good to eat    **D.** in the garden

_____ **10.** Once again Lapin needed to be
    **A.** cheered up    **C.** yelled at
    **B.** chewed up    **D.** called to

# U N I T
# 20

## Money Doctors

Have you ever ripped a dollar bill by mistake? If so, perhaps you taped it back together. But sometimes money is damaged in more serious ways. Then it is not as easy to fix. If you cannot repair paper money, you cannot use it. So you have to send badly damaged money to a special government office in Washington, D.C.

About twenty people work in this office. They sit at long tables under bright lights. Their main tools are magnifying glasses and tweezers. Their job is to piece together the damaged bills. The workers try to find at least half of each bill. Otherwise the government will not pay the owner for it.

This office is very busy. It handles up to forty thousand cases a year. People may wait six months before their case comes up. But it's worth it. The service is free, and you may get your money back.

---

**1.** If you cannot repair paper money, you cannot
   **A.** buy it       **C.** hide it
   **B.** use it       **D.** send it

**2.** You can send badly damaged money to a government
   **A.** bank       **C.** office
   **B.** bill       **D.** tool

**3.** The workers' main tools are magnifying glasses and
   **A.** tables       **C.** tweezers
   **B.** tape       **D.** lights

**4.** Workers find half of a bill so the government will
   **A.** pay the owner       **C.** call the owner
   **B.** fix the money       **D.** take the job

**5.** The services of this office are
   **A.** expensive       **C.** early
   **B.** free       **D.** easy

How is money damaged? Sometimes it is in a fire. Then a person may have mostly ashes to send in. Sometimes money is in a flood. Then the bills are faded and stuck together. People have sent money that had gone through the washing machine. Some bills have been chewed by animals. Others somehow got into blenders.

Also some people don't like banks. So they hide their money in unusual places. If bills are buried in cans, they sometimes get moldy. Mice often nibble at money hidden in attics and basements.

What is the biggest case so far? A truck carrying money for a bank exploded. There was a big fire. The truck company sent in the remains of the bills. They were worth two and a half million dollars. Thanks to the government workers, the company got a check for all the money.

---

_____ 6. When bills are burned, they turn to
   A. coins          C. dust
   B. ashes          D. sand

_____ 7. When bills get wet, they
   A. fade           C. fall
   B. burn           D. blend

_____ 8. Some people hide money because they don't like
   A. fires          C. mice
   B. checks         D. banks

_____ 9. The biggest case was about money burned in
   A. lightning      C. an explosion
   B. a basement     D. an airplane

_____ 10. Thanks to the workers, the company was able to
   A. put out the fire    C. get the money back
   B. write a check       D. buy the money back

# U N I T
# 21

## Robotics

Rebecca is a big help in her house. She carries things from one place to another. She can also open and close doors. And she never speaks unless someone speaks to her first. Rebecca does just what she is told to do, except when her batteries run down. Then Rebecca is no help at all, for Rebecca is a robot. Her heart is made of batteries, and her brain is a computer.

The English word *robot* comes from another language. The Latin word *robota* means work that is dull because it has to be done over and over. Robots are good for such jobs. They can be told to do the same thing again and again.

Rebecca is one of about ten thousand robots used in schools and homes in the United States. Many of these robots are owned by people who have computer hobbies. These people enjoy telling their robots to do useful tasks.

_____

1. Rebecca does what she is told, except when her
   A. lights are off
   B. door is closed
   C. batteries run down
   D. owner goes away

_____

2. Rebecca's heart is a
   A. brain
   B. battery
   C. light
   D. robot

_____

3. A word that means dull work done over and over is
   A. robota
   B. battery
   C. language
   D. program

_____

4. About ten thousand robots are used in schools and
   A. homes
   B. hotels
   C. hospitals
   D. libraries

_____

5. Many robot owners have computer
   A. jobs
   B. tasks
   C. stores
   D. hobbies

Many robots work in factories. These robots do jobs that are boring, hard, or dangerous for people to do. For instance, a robot might be a painter. Its job might be to paint car parts. Other robots drill holes.

Robots help in other jobs, too. Some robots make plastic food containers. Others work in food plants wrapping ice-cream bars. Still other robots make watches. These are perfect jobs for robots. Robots are best at doing the same job over and over.

The science of robots is called robotics. People who work in robotics are making robots for other purposes, too. They are building robots with TV cameras as eyes. Scientists hope that these robots will explore the bottom of the sea. Robots can go places that people can't.

---

_____ **6.** Robots do jobs that are boring, dangerous, or
  **A.** difficult     **C.** different
  **B.** clever     **D.** thoughtful

_____ **7.** A robot could paint
  **A.** pictures     **C.** houses
  **B.** car parts     **D.** faces

_____ **8.** Another job that robots do is
  **A.** drive cars     **C.** build factories
  **B.** wind watches     **D.** wrap ice-cream bars

_____ **9.** The study of robots is called
  **A.** mechanics     **C.** robotics
  **B.** acrobatics     **D.** bionics

_____ **10.** Scientists hope to use robots for
  **A.** seaside amusement     **C.** underwater adventures
  **B.** diving lessons     **D.** underwater exploration

Alur was a contented man. He had a beautiful wife and four cheerful children, and there were never any quarrels in his home.

One day Alur visited his old friend Gungu. Gungu was smoking a pipe, which was an unusual thing for him to do. "Why are you smoking a pipe?" asked Alur. "Well, my friend," answered Gungu, "the smoke from this pipe carries my troubles away." Alur asked, "What is *trouble*? I have never heard of it. It sounds exciting and interesting. I would like to obtain some of this *trouble*." Gungu was amazed. "You want *trouble*? No one wants that!" he said. Alur replied, "But I am curious! Please, Gungu, give me some of this *trouble* you've spoken of."

Gungu frowned, but he said to Alur, "If you insist, I will present you with a little *trouble*. Send your children here tomorrow afternoon to get some *trouble* for you."

---

_____ 1. In Alur's home there were never any
    A. quarrels     C. wives
    B. friends      D. children

_____ 2. Gungu was smoking
    A. a need      C. a fire
    B. a pipe      D. an idea

_____ 3. To Alur *trouble* sounded
    A. amazing    C. interesting
    B. terrible     D. contented

_____ 4. When he heard about *trouble*, Alur was
    A. unhappy    C. angry
    B. curious     D. smoking

_____ 5. Gungu asked Alur to send his
    A. wife       C. children
    B. home      D. pipe

The next day Gungu put a hummingbird into a box and wrapped it up. When Alur's children arrived, Gungu said, "Take this present to your father. It is the *trouble* he asked for."

The children had never heard of *trouble* either. As they walked home, they became curious about the contents of the box. They began to quarrel about whether they should open it. "I'll settle this!" said one child. He opened the box, and the hummingbird escaped. Now the children began to argue about whose fault it was that the bird had gotten away. When Alur came along to find his children, they were fighting and yelling.

Alur ran to Gungu's house and shouted, "What is this you have done, Gungu? My children never fought before!" Gungu replied, "Now you know what *trouble* is. And I hope you know something else now, too. Never think that something is wonderful just because you don't have it."

___

**6.** Gungu gave Alur's children a
  A. child        C. home
  B. pipe         D. hummingbird

**7.** The children became curious about
  A. Gungu        C. the present
  B. some boxes   D. their walk

**8.** When the hummingbird escaped, the children
  A. chased it    C. found their father
  B. called Gungu D. fought more

**9.** Alur saw that his children were
  A. unhappy      C. pleased
  B. injured      D. tired

**10.** After this experience Alur knew
  A. how birds fly   C. that Gungu was mean
  B. what trouble was D. where the bird went

Do you think that the North Pole and the South Pole are alike? Most people do. But in fact the two areas are quite different. The North Pole is in the Arctic Ocean. The South Pole lies near the center of Antarctica. Antarctica is colder than the Arctic. In fact, Antarctica is by far the coldest region on Earth.

One reason for Antarctica's very cold climate is that it has mountains high above sea level. Summers there rarely get above freezing. Ice and snow cover almost all of Antarctica throughout the entire year.

The Arctic region includes lands around the Arctic Ocean. The Arctic region is mostly at or near sea level. In parts of the Arctic, summers can be as warm as those in Boston. They just do not last as long. Most of the Arctic lands have no snow or ice in the summer.

_____ **1.** The North Pole is
    **A.** on land      **C.** in the Arctic Ocean
    **B.** on a mountain      **D.** in Antarctica

_____ **2.** Antarctica is the coldest
    **A.** region      **C.** city
    **B.** state      **D.** nation

_____ **3.** Antarctica has
    **A.** rivers      **C.** mountains
    **B.** sand      **D.** jungles

_____ **4.** The Arctic is the area around
    **A.** Boston      **C.** the South Pole
    **B.** Antarctica      **D.** the North Pole

_____ **5.** The Arctic is mostly
    **A.** in Boston      **C.** above sea level
    **B.** at sea level      **D.** below sea level

SCORE

Antarctica also has most of the world's permanent ice. The ice rests on land. Its average thickness is 8,000 feet. But ice in the Arctic rests on water. Its thickness varies from 10 to 65 feet.

If you traveled to the Arctic, you would see reindeer, polar bears, seals, birds, and insects. If your stay lasted through all the seasons, you might see over a thousand types of plants. You might also meet some of the people who live there. These people have learned to live in the cold climate quite well. They have been able to use the plants and animals there. Most of the people live near the sea, where they catch fish.

If you visited Antarctica, you would see ice and more ice. Very few animals and plants can live there. Most animals live on the coast. The largest animal that can live on the mainland is a small fly. And you would not see people at all, unless you ran into an explorer or a scientist.

_____

_____ **6.** In the Arctic, ice rests on
   A. ice               C. land
   B. plants            D. the ocean

_____ **7.** Compared to ice in the Arctic, ice in Antarctica is
   A. whiter            C. thicker
   B. smaller           D. thinner

_____ **8.** In the Arctic, you would see
   A. only ice          C. no animals
   B. no plants         D. many animals

_____ **9.** The largest animal on mainland Antarctica is a
   A. fly               C. polar bear
   B. fish              D. reindeer

_____ **10.** If you saw people in Antarctica, they might be
   A. farmers           C. digging up trees
   B. scientists        D. hunting reindeer

FACTS • LEVEL E                                    51

It seemed that Josephine Dickson hurt herself all the time. She often suffered from small cuts and burns. When she married Mr. Dickson in 1920, she was very happy. But she cut herself with a knife two times during the first week of their marriage. This worried Josephine, of course. It worried Mr. Dickson, too.

Mr. Dickson became even more worried when Josephine's habit did not stop. She had small accidents all the time. Mr. Dickson wanted to think of something that would help her. He worked for a company that made sticky tape and bandages. He thought that these things could help. But the bandages that the company made were very large. They were meant for hospitals to use. These bandages were too large for small cuts. Mr. Dickson wanted to make a smaller bandage that would be easy to put on and would stay in place.

_____ **1.** Josephine Dickson hurt herself
    **A.** rarely       **C.** once a month
    **B.** at night     **D.** all the time

_____ **2.** Josephine married Mr. Dickson in
    **A.** 1902       **C.** 1820
    **B.** 1912       **D.** 1920

_____ **3.** During the first week of her marriage, Josephine
    **A.** cried a lot     **C.** got a job
    **B.** cut herself     **D.** talked too much

_____ **4.** Mr. Dickson wanted to
    **A.** go away     **C.** laugh
    **B.** move       **D.** help

_____ **5.** Mr. Dickson's company made
    **A.** bandages     **C.** hospitals
    **B.** cuts       **D.** knives

SCORE

Mr. Dickson brought home some sticky tape and bandages. He cut the tape into strips about two inches long. Then he cut the bandages into small squares. He placed one square on each strip of tape. He then covered the sticky part of the tape with cloth. The cloth could easily be pulled off when the bandage was needed. From then on when Josephine cut herself, she could take care of the cut in a very short time.

The people at Mr. Dickson's company heard about his idea. They began making the new type of bandage. At first they made the bandages by hand, a few at a time. They didn't sell very many. Then the company began to give the new bandages away to Boy Scout troops. People began to use them often. Sales improved. Four years later, the company put in special machines to make the bandages. Today most people keep these "Band-Aids" in their homes.

_____

_____ 6. Mr. Dickson brought home some things from
    A. his work      C. the library
    B. a store      D. a doctor's office

_____ 7. Mr. Dickson used cloth, bandages, and
    A. tape      C. medicine
    B. troops      D. machines

_____ 8. The new bandage let Josephine take care of cuts
    A. on walks      C. at Mr. Dickson's office
    B. quickly      D. in two hours

_____ 9. The people at Mr. Dickson's company
    A. laughed      C. ignored him
    B. liked his idea      D. made fun of him

_____ 10. People found that the new bandages were
    A. too small      C. useful
    B. strange      D. too sticky

# The Eyes Have It

Try an experiment. Hold your arms out to your sides. Extend your index fingers and slowly bring your arms together in front of you. Try to make your fingers touch. Since that was so easy, try it again with only one eye open.

If you are like most people, the task is more challenging using only one eye. There is a reason for this. A certain signal goes to your brain when you look at objects with both eyes. This signal tells your brain how close or how far away objects are. If you use only one eye, your brain does not receive this signal. You cannot judge distance correctly or tell how thick objects are. You have lost your ability to see depth. When you look at objects with one eye, your brain "sees" the scene as if it were painted on a flat screen. Using two eyes gives depth to the same view.

_____ 1. You begin the experiment by holding your arms
    A. behind you     C. out to your sides
    B. above your head   D. down by your sides

_____ 2. Next you bring your arms
    A. down     C. behind your head
    B. up     D. in front of you

_____ 3. It is easiest to make your fingers meet if you have
    A. good luck     C. one eye closed
    B. good vision     D. both eyes open

_____ 4. To judge distance, use
    A. one eye     C. your arms
    B. both eyes     D. your fingers

_____ 5. When you use one eye, the brain "sees"
    A. a flat scene     C. only large things
    B. far away     D. only small things

Each of your eyes sees things from a slightly different angle. Your left eye sees more of the objects to your left, and your right eye sees more of the objects to your right. Try another experiment. Look at a nearby object with one eye closed, and notice what you can see. Then close the other eye and look at the same object. How does this change what you see? Now look with both eyes. When you have both eyes open, each eye sees not only the front of the object but also a little on each side.

This special vision is called depth perception. Depth perception makes you able to judge distances. It helps you avoid running into things. It helps you catch a ball. Newborn babies do not have this ability. It takes a few years for it to develop. That is why some children who have trouble in sports become wonderful athletes later.

_____ **6.** Each of your eyes sees things from a different
    **A.** angle         **C.** signal
    **B.** nerve         **D.** light

_____ **7.** Your left eye sees more of the objects
    **A.** to the left         **C.** to the center
    **B.** to the right         **D.** to the front

_____ **8.** When both your eyes are open, they
    **A.** work less         **C.** stand apart
    **B.** see more         **D.** work harder

_____ **9.** Depth perception makes you able to judge
    **A.** angles         **C.** eyes
    **B.** color         **D.** distances

_____ **10.** Depth perception is well developed in
    **A.** children         **C.** athletes
    **B.** newborns         **D.** objects

# *Think and Apply*

## *Fact Finding*

Study the part of the telephone directory below. It shows facts from the yellow pages. Use the facts to answer the questions.

| |
|---|
| **Party Planning Services** |
| **Clowns, Clowns, Clowns!** |
| 12 River Street ..........................................................**555-8347** |
| **Magic Maria Party Shows** |
| 1302 Congress Street, Room 192 ............................**555-0010** |
| **Singing Telegrams** |
| 537 West Union Street .........................................**555-9476** |
| **Party Supplies, Rental** |
| **Costumes, Inc.** |
| 75 Maple Blvd. .....................................................**555-9000** |
| **Favors and Fun** |
| 10 Market Street ..................................................**555-5352** |
| **Party Rentals** |
| 964 River Street ...................................................**555-8772** |

1. You want a magician to perform at a birthday party. What number will you call? _____

2. You're invited to a costume party, and you want an unusual disguise. What is the name of the company you will call?

   _____

3. You want to see a selection of party favors. What is the address of the shop you will go to? _____

4. You have rented some chairs for a party. To what street will you go to pick them up? _____

5. You call 555-9476. What service are you interested in?

   _____

6. You think that you would like to be a clown for parties. What number will you call for information? _____

**To check your answers, turn to page 62.**

## *Listing Facts*

List at least three facts you need to know in order to complete each task.

**A.** Mail out the invitations to a party.

  **1.** _____

  **2.** _____

  **3.** _____

**B.** Pack for a trip to your cousin's house.

  **1.** _____

  **2.** _____

  **3.** _____

**C.** Pick up a friend on the way to a basketball game.

  **1.** _____

  **2.** _____

  **3.** _____

**D.** Go to the doctor.

  **1.** _____

  **2.** _____

  **3.** _____

**E.** Buy a birthday present.

  **1.** _____

  **2.** _____

  **3.** _____

## Just the Facts, Please!

Newspaper reporters give facts in their stories. They try to answer six main questions. **Who** was involved? **What** happened? **When** did it happen? **Where** did it happen? **Why** did it happen? **How** did it happen?

Pretend that you are a reporter for a newspaper. Write a story about a lion that escaped from the zoo. In your story try to answer the six questions.

### Lion Escapes from Zoo!

_____

_____

_____

_____

_____

_____

_____

_____

_____

_____

_____

_____

_____